D1461322

BELLA YOUNGER'S

Deliciously

STELLA

VIKING

an imprint of

PENGUIN BOOKS

VIKING

UK | USA | Canada | Ireland | Australia
India | New Zealand | South Africa

Viking is part of the Penguin Random House group of companies
whose addresses can be found at global.penguinrandomhouse.com.

Penguin
Random House
UK

First published 2016
001

Set in League Script and Brandon Grotesque
Colour reproduction by BORN
Printed in Italy by LEGO

A CIP catalogue record for this book is available from the British Library

ISBN: 978-0-241-25756-2

www.greenpenguin.co.uk

MIX
Paper from
responsible sources
FSC® C018179

Penguin Random House is committed to a
sustainable future for our business, our readers
and our planet. This book is made from Forest
Stewardship Council® certified paper.

TO MY FAMILY,
WHO HAVE
ENDURED ME
THE LONGEST.

Introduction

Dear reader,

Thank you so much for buying my book. As you turn the pages, I ask you to inhale deeply and take in the paper's smell; this is the smell of a more beautiful, radiant and energized you. This book brings together all the recipes and ingredients that I love, and the secrets to my beautiful life. I wrote this book with love, and if cooking these recipes gives you half as much joy as I take in sharing them with you, I'll be glowing on the inside and out.

People are always asking me how I'm able to maintain my smoking-hot bod and radiant sparkle. I used to think it was down to genetics. My grandmother always said that I would age well because I've had an easy life, but now I am sure that the real secret to my success is my unique diet and inspirational approach to health.

Now, I know what some of you might be thinking: who is this girl? How has she achieved such influence and what does she know about wellness? If I'm honest with you, I'm not sure. I am not a chef nor am I a nutritionist. All I know is that I have a story to tell and a larger-than-average following on Instagram. I often think that young, middle-class white women are under-represented in the health industry. With this book I hope to redress that balance and help you to nourish your body from the inside out.

My food journey began on a day when I had eaten a packet of Hula-Hoops for breakfast on the way to work and somebody had sneezed in my hair on the Underground. I was a vile, fat wretch who ate all the wrong food, all the time. My hair was dry, my skin was dull, I didn't look good in a gym kit. In short, I appeared to be a lost cause.

That day, I searched #inspo on Instagram for four solid hours and, just as I was walking to the fridge, I caught my reflection in a nearby mirror. I asked myself, 'What do you see?' A pig in a wig stared back.

I knew then that something had to be done. I needed a lifestyle overhaul and fast. I also knew that I couldn't do it alone. I started my Instagram account, Deliciously Stella, in the hope that I could share my progress and the delicious food I found along the way with my close friends. I never imagined that so many of you would join me on my journey as I rediscovered the sugar highs of WKD Blue and the comforting warmth of melted cheese. I truly cannot express my gratitude that you did, and I know that with time and dedication, the results will speak for themselves. All things happen for a reason, and my reason, readers, is you.

Top Five Tips

FOR GETTING STARTED

LISTEN TO YOUR BODY, NOT YOUR DOCTOR

I may not be a scientist, but I think I know enough about modern medicine to know that it is obsolete. From working closely with my mum's nutritionist, who has a GCSE in science and has done a course, I have learned there is no illness that can't be cured by changing your diet. If cleansing your colon with a daily purple juice makes you feel good, then it's likely that it can cure cancer as well.

NOBODY LIKES A QUITTER

The most important thing I have learned about sticking with dietary changes is *not* to focus on what you're giving up, but to instead fixate on all the exciting new ingredients that you'll be arranging in bowls. Your followers are there to support you on this journey, but they are also there to judge you. Luckily social media is the perfect place to construct a seemingly perfect life, so you can strike the perfect balance between inspiring and smug.

MONEY IS NO OBJECT

Health foods can be expensive, but if you're really committed to this lifestyle you will find a way to afford it. If you are struggling to find the money to make positive food choices, I suggest robbing a bank or burning this book in shame.

SURROUND YOURSELF WITH LIKE-MINDED PEOPLE

Statistics have shown that people are more likely to stick to a diet (ugh, I hate that word) if they have a buddy. If you surround yourself with people who think exactly the same as you do then no one will question your teachings, or try to disrupt your new, healthy lifestyle.

POSSIBLE SIDE EFFECTS

When you first start on your journey, it's likely that you will feel different, but this isn't a cause for concern. Common side effects of your new lifestyle may include: talking about yourself, trying to convert people to your new way of life, taking gym selfies, using inspirational quotes, constantly Instagramming the food you are about to consume, and a general sense of self-importance.

YOU

CANT

MILK

AN

ALMOND

How to Cook Clean
WHEN YOU'RE NOT A CHEF

One of the first things people ask me when they hear about my lifestyle is, 'How did you learn to cook?' You might be surprised to hear that the answer is, 'I didn't.' The thing I'm most proud of about this book is that the recipes require no discernible chef skills. As long as you can heat things up and arrange ingredients in bowls, then with a little practice you should soon become as talented a chef as I am. If you want to use a trial-and-error approach to these dishes, that's fine too. Even I'm not sure if they work properly and I wrote them!

No one was more surprised than my friends when I said that I was writing a cookbook. Before I started on this journey I couldn't boil an egg, let alone devise a series of delicious pasta alternatives. I wasn't thinking about what I was putting in my body at all and I paid no attention to what was in my ingredients and where they were from. If I can make these dishes, anyone can!

Always Make Sure
THAT YOUR INGREDIENTS
ARE LOCALLY SOURCED

CORNER SHOPS

My mantra has always been 'The closer it is to your kitchen, the better it is for your body', so I always make sure that I source my ingredients from shops as close to my front doorstep as possible. My nearest shop is a corner shop called Shop Express and it has an excellent sweet selection. The man who runs it is Turkish so there's the added bonus of exotic foods as well. It's good to develop a relationship with the owner of your corner shop. That way they'll let you know when the rarer ingredients are in stock. (Purple gummy bears are a favourite.)

PICK YOUR OWN

Being able to pick your own ingredients is one of life's greatest gifts and nothing brings a smile to my face like a trip to my local pick 'n' mix. Since Woolworths closed down it's been harder to find good pick 'n' mix but my top tip is to go to a cinema. The produce is rare so it can be quite expensive, but it's worth it because the range is so great.

Frequently Asked QUESTIONS

CAN I EAT OUT WITH FRIENDS AND STILL STICK TO MY DIET?

The answer to this is, thankfully, yes. Unless you are in a juice bar or a raw, vegan restaurant you should be able to find healthy food wherever you are. If you're struggling you can always ask the kitchen to arrange some ingredients in a bowl for you – it shouldn't be too much trouble.

WHEN WILL I START TO SEE RESULTS?

This lifestyle is as much about a change of thinking as it is about a change of diet. If you think you can see the results, then you will see them. My grandmother always said that horses sweat, gentlemen perspire and ladies glow; jumping in a sauna is a great way to see your new-found shine on the outside while also feeling it on the inside.

WHY IS THERE NO TOFU IN THIS BOOK?

Tofu is disgusting.

Breakfast

Before I started on my food journey, breakfast wasn't really on my radar. If I managed to eat in the morning, it would usually be when I was in the shower, and I don't need to warn you of the dangers of waterlogged toast. Failing that, it would be an expensive take-out or even a packet of crisps – not exactly a beautiful start to the day. Now I know that breakfast is the most important meal of the day, and that it's important to sit down and savour it. Breakfast is your first chance to fill your body with nutritious energy for the day ahead and I'm confident that these recipes are the best way to do that. It's also one of my favourite meals because so many of the best breakfast dishes are arranged in bowls.

In this chapter you'll learn how to make perfect poached eggs and warming porridge the Stella way, with simple wholesome ingredients and recipes that are so easy, you might not even think they're recipes. Glistening green juices and scrummy smoothies are the order of the day as I help you find the balance between delicious and nutritious.

Avocado & Eggs
ON TOAST
THREE WAYS

Did you know that avocado and eggs on toast is the most photographed food on Instagram? It's easy to see why. Avocados are full of fat and their green colour means that they look great with a filter. Getting your eggs to look perfect can be tricky but once you know these easy life hacks you'll never look back. There are loads of delicious pre-packaged poached eggs to choose from but these three never let me down. Remember, the more love you give your eggs the more you'll get back.

SERVES 2

INGREDIENTS

2 slices bread

2 avocados

1 bag gummy eggs/2 Crème Eggs/2 large value scotch eggs

METHOD

Open the bag of ready-sliced bread and put 2 slices in the toaster for 2.5 minutes. You'll want the toast to be crisp and brown. Mash the avocados together in a bowl until you get a paste that has the consistency of guacamole but none of the extra flavourings. Slather all over the freshly toasted bread. Then arrange your chosen ready-made eggs on top with a squeeze of lemon or a sprinkle of chilli flakes. If you want the perfect poached egg effect, I recommend starting with gummy eggs, but many other pre-prepared eggs will give you a similarly great result.

etting your eggs to look perfect can be tricky but once you know these easy life hacks you'll never look back.

Club Tropicana
PORRIDGE

I have two favourite sayings in life: 'Worse things have happened at sea' and 'Everything should remind you of George Michael'. This delicious, nourishing porridge is like having a cocktail for breakfast, and who doesn't want an excuse to start drinking before their commute? I especially love to eat it on holiday because it looks great against the backdrop of the sea and it gets me loosened up before a day of upside down selfies on the sun lounger – no one needs to know you're not really doing beach yoga!

SERVES 1

INGREDIENTS

1 mug porridge oats

1 glass Malibu coconut rum

2 foam bananas

3 sour strawberries

4 gummy melons

3 gummy pineapples

1 cocktail umbrella

METHOD

Mix the porridge oats and the Malibu together in a bowl until you reach a consistency similar to that of wallpaper paste. My special tip is not to heat the porridge up; that way you won't burn off any of the alcohol and miss out on that lovely coconut flavour. You should really be able to smell the rum as the oats soak it up. This will probably make you feel like dancing. Malibu always makes me feel like dancing. Pat down the porridge mixture to create a flat surface, then carefully arrange the gummy fruits on top. Make sure you leave space for the cocktail umbrella, and *voilà*! You've made Jamaica in a bowl.

Warming Nut Butter
PORRIDGE

Porridge and winter go together like me and wine – a dream come true. I am such a nut butter addict. It's so healthy and full of protein, and you can eat it with anything. My friends always tease me when they catch me eating it straight out of the food processor but it's worth the slap on the wrist. What they don't know is that nut butter is a totally guilt-free treat. The chocolatey nutty toppings make this porridge as indulgent as a pudding and, for me, it's the perfect stress buster. Remember, stressed is desserts spelled backwards!

SERVES 2

INGREDIENTS

1 mug porridge oats

1 cup cow's milk

3 tsp peanut butter chocolate spread

A handful of cacao chips

A handful of chocolate-covered nuts

METHOD

Top secret Stella tip: Lots of people use cacao in their healthy recipes but it's really just a fancy word for chocolate. Chocolate is full of antioxidants, which have been proven to lengthen your life and even cure tennis elbow.

Warm the oats and milk in a pan until they reach the consistency of warm wallpaper paste. This is a winter porridge so you'll want it to be warm. When you're heating the oats, don't forget to stir them. It's important to stir things when they're heating up. When the oats start to steam, pour them into a beautiful bowl and stir in your peanut butter chocolate so that you can see a delicious swirl. Arrange the chocolate chips and chocolate-covered nuts on top, then you'll have porridge fit for a squirrel.

Summer Berry
PORRIDGE

Raspberries are one of my favourite fruits and they're definitely the star attraction in this delicious porridge. They're also jam-packed full of vitamins and can double up as a beautiful lip stain. Some of you might not think that porridge is a recipe but I believe that a different topping makes a different dish. When I first started eating clean, I had one go-to porridge recipe. Now I can make at least three different porridge recipes and each one is more delicious than the last. Make a note of all the different toppings you use. You might be surprised by how many recipes you have in your repertoire.

SERVES 1

INGREDIENTS

1 cup cow's milk

1 packet strawberry sherbet

1 mug porridge oats

1 bottle strawberry sauce

5 gummy raspberries

5 gummy blackberries

1 packet popping candy

METHOD

Warm the milk with the strawberry sherbet until it is infused. The milk should turn a slightly alarming pink colour, a bit like Pepto-Bismol. Stir in the oats until you have a consistency that looks like slurry. Although this is a summer porridge, you'll want it to be warm so it doesn't feel like cold sick slipping down your throat. Pour the mixture into a bowl then stir in the strawberry sauce in an anticlockwise motion to create a lovely swirl. Arrange the gummy berries on top of the porridge then sprinkle with the popping candy, which adds a much-needed zing for an extra boost on a busy morning.

Sprinkle with the popping candy, which adds a much-needed zing for an extra boost on a busy morning.

#

IJUST

DONTWANT

TOLOOKBACK

ANDTHINKI

COULDHAVE

EATENTHAT

Finding green food that tastes yummy in liquid form can prove very, very difficult.

Glistening Green
BREAKFAST SMOOTHIE

Like most people, I have a cupboard in my kitchen known as the kitchen gadget graveyard, where candy floss makers and yoghurt machines go to die. I don't often use my Nutribullet, but when it comes to this delicious recipe, there really is nothing better for the job.

Finding green food that tastes yummy in liquid form can prove very, very difficult. That's why I can't sing the praises of food colouring enough. I didn't eat much food colouring when I was growing up because my sister is allergic to it, so I'm making up for lost time now by using it to make delicious green juices as often as possible. Dyeing things green automatically makes them look healthy, so don't be afraid to use this fantastic ingredient liberally. Just make sure you always have some stashed away for a rainy day!

SERVES 1

INGREDIENTS

1 cup sugar

2 cups water

2 cups ice

5 to 10 drops green food colouring

2 shots apple liqueur

METHOD

Pour all the ingredients into the Nutribullet and blast. This juice works in every shade of green so feel free to add more or less food colouring, depending on whether you want a zesty lime colour or a subtle bilge colour. The juice should be the consistency of a slush puppy and taste very sweet, with an added zing of apple, thanks to the liqueur. Pour the mixture into a jam jar so everyone can see that your juice is green, then add a straw. You'll be feeling self-righteous all day!

BEAUTIFUL
Berry Blast
BREAKFAST SMOOTHIE

This beautiful berry blast is packed full of skin-glowing vitamin E and will nourish you from the inside out. Popping candy is nature's multitasker and it adds a much-needed zing to any dish. I always try to start the day with a spoonful of this magic to get me off to a fizzing start; sometimes I can feel it popping away all day.

The arrangement of this dish can be tricky but it's worth making the effort for the end result. Lots of people find dairy difficult to digest and nobody wants to overdose on calcium. If you are avoiding dairy products then condensed milk is a brilliant alternative. No one will doubt your commitment to health with a dish as pretty as this.

SERVES 2

INGREDIENTS

4 gummy strawberries

1 tin condensed milk

2 tsp strawberry jam

4 gummy blackberries

1 packet popping candy

METHOD

Line 2 jam jars with the strawberries so that you can see them through the glass. If you're going to make the effort to eat healthy fruit, it's important to make sure other people can see you doing it. Pour the condensed milk and the strawberry jam into the jam jars, being careful not to disturb the gummy strawberries. Top the smoothies with gummy blackberries and a spoonful of popping candy. Trust me – your body will thank you for it.

Soups & Salads

Soups and salads are the perfect light lunch and a food for all seasons. Nothing is more warming than a piping hot bowl of soup in the colder months, and nothing beats the crisp bite of a healthy summer salad. The key to their success is colour. A vibrant, colourful soup or salad is a tasty soup or salad, and the most important thing to remember is to use fresh, organic ingredients to make those beautiful bowls sing. Locally sourced produce is a must, so get yourself down to your local corner shop and buy some beautiful, colourful food.

Soups are a great option when you're on a detox or cleanse, and salads are the perfect summer meal staple. They also make for a wonderful packed lunch when you're on the go. Soups and salads can be pre-prepared and assembled in seconds so you'll have plenty of time for yoga, recipe testing and walking your dog.

Blueberry and CUCUMBER SALAD

This recipe is all about flavour. The juniper and quinine dressing really makes the blueberries and cucumber sing. My golden rule is to always have ice in the freezer. This salad is best served chilled and is great for keeping cool on long summer days in the park. Gin is amazing for digestion and really gives your skin a beautiful glow. This salad also makes a great light supper before a big night out. It keeps me dancing all night long.

SERVES 1

INGREDIENTS

4 strips cucumber
6 blueberries
2 shots gin
1 bottle tonic water

METHOD

Use a potato peeler to peel strips off a cucumber and arrange them in a glass tumbler. Scatter the blueberries on top and then add the ice. Pour 2 shots of gin over the ice. You should hear a satisfying crackle when the liquid hits the ice. Then top up the dressing with the tonic water to give it a quinine kick, and you've got a beautiful summer salad that's healthy and impressive.

Seafood SURPRISE

When I started writing this book I thought long and hard about whether to include fish in my recipes. Although I am technically vegetarian, I make an exception for fish so that I can make this delicious broth. Luckily goldfish can be locally sourced from fairgrounds and, as they're not in the sea, they can't be overfished. Using sustainably sourced food and environmentally friendly produce is incredibly important to me – that's why I only buy fish that I can find within a five mile radius of my home.

SERVES 2

INGREDIENTS

1 carton goldfish crackers

1 pack gummy fish

METHOD

Empty the carton of goldfish crackers into a bowl. I think it's best to use a blue tablecloth, so that the fish look like they could be in the sea. Make sure that all the goldfish crackers are still whole, so that the dish remains in keeping with its nautical theme. Carefully pick your chosen gummy fish and hide them amongst the goldfish for a delicious surprise. Arrange some on the top of the bowl and serve.

Top tip alert: Gummy fish are completely gluten free so this dish is a wonderful option if you're pretending to be a coeliac.

Goldfish can be locally sourced from fairgrounds and, as they're not in the sea, they can't be overfished.

Brussels Sprout
SALAD

This sprout dish is a health-packed powerhouse. Some people think that sprouts are only available at Christmas but I like them to play a key part in my summer cooking. The sprouts you're used to eating will be vegetable sprouts but these summer sprouts are much more delicious. Typical Christmas sprouts can have a distinctive bin-juice flavour, so I think it's best to avoid them. Stock up on these beauties from October, but store them up to use all year round.

SERVES 2

INGREDIENTS

1 box of Choc on Choc Brussels sprouts

2 bags Marks & Spencer chocolate Brussels sprouts

METHOD

Skewer the net bag with a pair of scissors or a knife, if you prefer. Be careful when using scissors or knives because they are sharp, second only in danger to the spiralizer, which once spiralized my finger. Once you have removed the outer net, arrange the sprouts in a bowl, being careful to remember not to remove their casing. They look much better when they're shiny and green. Try to build a small sprout tower; this will help your salad look plentiful and will give the impression that the diner should be full after eating it.

Protein-Packed
KALE SALAD

This salad is great because it really makes the finger-licking chicken the star of the meal. Fried chicken is my absolute favourite food because it is deep fat fried and locally sourced from the chicken shop just down the road from my house. Kale is sometimes criticized for soaking up toxins from the soil, but in this salad all it is soaking up is delicious, salty fat. This is a great salad to take to work or enjoy with friends – a real multitasker.

SERVES 4

INGREDIENTS

50g kale

1 pat butter

1 family bucket fried chicken

A splash of tomato ketchup

METHOD

Chop the kale roughly into small strips and massage it gently with half the butter. This gives it a rich, salty taste that really complements its earthy texture. Fry the kale in the other half of the butter and then arrange it in a bowl. Take the pieces of deep fried chicken out of the family bucket and arrange them in the bowl so that they completely cover the kale. Drizzle the salad with tomato ketchup and you're left with a beautiful dish that can feed the whole family.

Croutons contain a lot of saturated fat so in this dish I use marshmallows as an alternative, because they're so light and energizing.

French Sucre
SOUP

I first tried this delicious soup in Paris and I've been dying to get the recipe right ever since. It's sweeter than most soups but I think it works perfectly as an *amuse-bouche* before one of my nourishing light salads. Croutons contain a lot of saturated fat so in this dish I use marshmallows as an alternative, because they're so light and energizing. Every sip will taste like liquid health and your whole body will be glowing from the inside out. I never use any milk other than cow's milk because dairy is delicious and I like the cows to feel needed. Make sure that your cow's milk is locally sourced from your closest supermarket so you're supporting businesses in your local area.

SERVES 1

INGREDIENTS

½ pint full fat milk

8 squares dark chocolate

25 marshmallows

METHOD

Simmer the milk in a pan over a low heat. Make sure you use a pan made of metal and not wood so it does not catch on fire and ruin your soup. Gradually add the chocolate to the warm milk, being careful to make sure that it melts into the liquid as you stir. You should stir both clockwise and anticlockwise to get the best results. For tips on stirring, you can look at my online tutorial or buy my next book on techniques. When the chocolate milk concoction is hot, arrange the marshmallows on the top in the shape of the Eiffel Tower. *Très Parisienne.*

SOUP

Cheese is one of my favourite foods and one of the main things that stops me from being a vegan. What some people don't realize is that cheese works really well in a soup. It melts really easily and, as an added bonus, most cheeses are completely gluten free. It's great because it's light, healthy and, most importantly, delicious.

This alpine soup is one of my absolute favourites because it tastes like winter and it goes fantastically well with white bread. It's also brilliant for sharing. I like to make it when I'm entertaining potential suitors because it's so sexy when you get cheese string on your chin.

SERVES 4

INGREDIENTS

1 loaf white bread

500g Gruyère cheese

1 cup white wine

1 shot sherry

METHOD

Chop the bread into cubes and put it in a basket. Melt the cheese in a pan until it has a molten, soup-like consistency. Gradually add the wine and sherry until you can smell the scent of booze rising like steam from the pan. I absolutely love recipes that use booze because you can drink straight from the bottle as you cook. Cheese is yellow, and yellow foods have been scientifically proven to fight off scurvy. Alcohol has been used as an antiseptic for generations and is brilliant for cleansing the system. Serve the soup in a sharing bowl with long forks to dip the bread. This is the definition of a winter warmer.

Cheese is yellow, and yellow foods have been scientifically proven to fight off scurvy.

LIFES TOO SHORT FOR SHAME

Summery
FRUIT SALAD

Summer is my favourite season because it's sunny, and my favourite thing to eat when it's sunny is fruit salad. This fruit salad is so easy, it takes almost no effort to make. All you need to do is make a quick trip to your local pick 'n' mix market and you're good to go. If I've got time, I like to go and check out what's available at my local cinema as their seasonal produce is excellent. Wilkinsons will probably have a good selection as well, and you can always swap in more plentiful fruits if you aren't able to get the full list of ingredients. Remember to use your most attractive bowl for arranging. You never know who might stumble across your photos on social media!

SERVES 2

INGREDIENTS

5 foam bananas

5 sour cherries

5 gummy strawberries

5 gummy melons

1 coconut chocolate bar

METHOD

Arrange your ingredients in a bowl, Instagram and enjoy!

Wintry Cinnamon-
AND CLOVE-SPICED SOUP

I love this soup recipe because it reminds me of Christmas, and nothing gets me excited like the thought of getting festively plump. I like to stretch my stomach in the lead up to the big day so I can eat as many pigs in blankets as possible, and as part of my preparation I always find myself drinking bucket loads of this soup. The oranges add much-needed vitamin C, so it's a brilliant way to avoid getting scurvy. The redcurrant jelly is a secret tip passed down to me by my mad grandmother; it really helps to get your dopamine levels up.

SERVES 3

INGREDIENTS

2 oranges

10 cloves

1 bottle cheap red wine

1 stick of cinnamon

4 tbsp sugar

2 tbsp redcurrant jelly

METHOD

Chop up the oranges and dot the skins with the cloves so they look like tiny orange hedgehogs. Put them in a pan and pour over the cheap red wine. Bring the wine to a simmer and add the cinnamon and sugar. Be careful not to let the liquid boil as you'll lose out on crucial boozy goodness. Remove from the heat when the sugar has dissolved. My secret tip is to sweeten this soup with some redcurrant jelly; this adds extra fruity vitamins and a delicious tangy taste. What a winter winner!

Top tip: The spices in this soup boost your immune system and your metabolism so you needn't look for an excuse to tuck into this warming broth.

Nothing gets me excited like the thought of getting festively plump.

Snacks

A lot of people think that to eat healthily you have to remove snacks from your daily meal plan, but I assure you this is not the case. Eating constantly is a great way to remind your metabolism to keep going, and you can't take your supplements on an empty stomach. Snacks also stop you slipping into an energy dip between meals. Sugary snacks will raise your blood sugar levels so it's important to make informed choices before you reach for the nearest edible item.

The key to snacking when you're eating clean is to prepare everything in advance. Tupperware is one of the best things ever to happen to healthy eating because it means we no longer need to reach for a chocolate bar when we're out and about. Even 'healthy' shop-bought snacks are often full of additives so don't fall into the trap of relying on them! In this chapter you'll learn how to make simple, nourishing snacks to keep you at your best self all day long.

Popcorn

It feels like you can't move for popcorn nowadays. It's such a brilliant, healthy alternative to crisps and it's so yummy. Toffee popcorn is my favourite variety because they've really nailed the sticky, energizing sauce. I used to like eating my popcorn drizzled with melted butter but since I've embraced the healthy life I've found it's just as delicious served straight from the pack.

SERVES 2

INGREDIENTS

1 sharing bag toffee popcorn

METHOD

Open the bag of popcorn. It should smell deliciously sweet and make a crunchy sound between your teeth. Pour the contents into 2 bowls, making sure to share it equally. This popcorn is so good it's easy to get in a fight if you feel short-changed by the division of the portions.

This popcorn is best enjoyed as a snack on the go, as a sweet treat after a meal or as a healthy side to any delicious supper.

Nut Butter
COOKIES

These delicious cookies are an absolute go-to of mine because they're super scrummy and so easy to make. Nut butter is so healthy and delicious and I'm sure this recipe will satisfy your sweet tooth. The cacao in the spread packs a much-needed punch of energy and antioxidants. It can be quite a messy business sandwiching the cookies together but it is well worth the effort. I like to pack these cookies for long journeys, and they also make a great snack when I'm on the go. They're so good I nearly always eat the whole tray.

SERVES 8

INGREDIENTS

1 packet chocolate-chip cookies
1 tub peanut butter chocolate spread

METHOD

Unwrap the cookies and arrange them in pairs on a tray. Open the tub of peanut butter chocolate spread and use a teaspoon to measure out a generous serving of the nut butter. Spread the nut butter on one cookie in each pair, and then use the other cookie in the pair to create a sandwich. Neaten up the edges with a pallet knife and arrange the sandwiches in a bowl. Don't worry if you make a mess at first. Nut butter is notorious for getting everywhere; sometimes I even find it in my hair.

Stella's Comforting
CHOCOLATE LOAF

White bread is one of my favourite carbs because it's healthy, natural and, of course, it's absolutely delicious. I'm a total nut butter addict so chocolate nut butter is one of my go-to everyday snacks. It's so yummy, I sometimes eat it on its own straight out of the jar, but it really sings in this comforting chocolate loaf. This loaf is what I eat whenever I'm feeling like I don't have the energy to spiralize some fresh veggies, and it always gets me in the mood for doing handstands.

SERVES 6

INGREDIENTS

1 loaf sliced plain white bread

1 extra-large tub chocolate nut butter

METHOD

Take a bag of plain white sliced bread and separate the pieces, placing them on a clean work surface in front of you. Don't worry about how it looks yet; when I first started working with bread I got crumbs everywhere, but you'll soon learn how to take the bread out of the packet without too much mess! Spread the chocolate nut butter carefully on both sides of each piece of bread, being careful not to spread it on the two end pieces – they are there to hold your loaf together. Carefully press the pieces of bread together, slowly reforming the loaf. The chocolate nut butter should stick the slices together nicely. When you are finished, you'll have a delicious, nourishing nut butter tower.

Energy
BITES

Energy bites are what I turn to when I need a pick-me-up on the go because they're an excellent source of healthy fats and, of course, energy. You can keep them in the fridge for healthy snacking throughout the day or pack some in a Tupperware container to eat while you're out and about. These balls of flavour work brilliantly as a pre- or post-workout snack. I've also heard that they're great for the 'mid-afternoon slump'. I don't know what it is like to work at a desk because I do yoga and have my photo taken all day but I've heard that the 'mid-afternoon desk slump' can be really draining. Hopefully these bites will help you get your sparkle back.

SERVES 1

INGREDIENTS

1 chocolate bar with a soft centre

1 pack spherical sweets / A handful of desiccated coconut

METHOD

Unwrap your chocolate bar and break it into pieces. Put the pieces in a blender and blend until you have a pliable mixture. Roll teaspoon-sized helpings of the mixture into perfect spheres. A lot of people like to decorate their energy balls with goji berries, but I find that they taste like tiny red pellets of hell so I prefer to use spherical sweets. They're sweeter and more spherical than goji berries but I think they work just as well. Use your palm to roll the spheres in the spherical sweets for a tangy berry flavour, or use the desiccated coconut if you fancy something sweeter.

Orange
BOWL

Some people might say that a dish with two ingredients doesn't require a recipe but I beg to differ. This Orange Bowl is one of my go-to showstoppers. It comes in a fancy shiny wrapper, so it's a great choice if you're trying to impress guests. Oranges are full of vitamin C and a chocolate orange is a great way to incorporate one of your five-a-day into a busy schedule of eating out and yoga practice. The tiny clementines are wonderfully tangy and so versatile. If you don't fancy eating them on their own, they work really well as part of a delicious summery fruit salad or even as an alternative to ice in a boozy cocktail.

SERVES 1

INGREDIENTS

1 chocolate orange

1 bag Marks & Spencer's chocolate clementines

METHOD

This is one of my all-time favourite recipes because you get to use two of my favourite pieces of kitchen equipment: a hammer and a screwdriver. To start, you remove the chocolate orange from its package, aim the screwdriver right in the centre of the top of the orange and hit it with the hammer. This 'tap and unwrap' motion should leave you with perfectly separated segments that you can arrange in a perfect circle. Scatter the edge of the bowl with the tiny chocolate clementines, keeping them in their wrappers for a splash of colour.

A chocolate orange is a great way to incorporate one of your five-a-day into a busy schedule of eating out and yoga practice.

Seedy Energy
BARS

Do you ever find that you hit an after-work slump at about 4 p.m.? I know I used to. I would reach for the same boring old chocolate over and over again. Eventually I realized that my snack choices really weren't challenging me. Everyone's been talking about the health benefits of seeds and seedy snacks so I decided to create my own take on this delicious snack trend. These seedy energy bars will keep you on your toes because you never know which one you're going to get. Nothing keeps me engaged at work like the prospect of a biscuit with a flasher on the front!

SERVES 8

INGREDIENTS

6 gingerbread men
A variety of cake decorations

METHOD

Carefully arrange the gingerbread men on a plate. Pipe seedy pictures on to them using the cake decoration set. My favourite design is of a man in a trench coat, but you can play around with whatever feels most seedy to you. If you're not very artistic, I've got loads of seedy stencils on my website for you to download.

Play around with whatever feels most seedy to you.

Crispbread

I love crispbread because it is a brilliant healthy alternative to bread. Bread is full of gluten, causes bloating and, at worst, can make your gut leak. Crispbread works really well as a healthy snack, but it is best when you're hungover as it's full of tasty salt. The most important thing to remember when you are making crispbread is to really compact those crisps so that they don't fall out of the sandwich. Again, with this recipe, practice makes perfect so take your time to get it right.

SERVES 1

INGREDIENTS

2 slices white bread

20g salted butter

1 packet salted crisps

METHOD

Take the slices of bread and generously cover them in the butter with a knife. Empty your packet of crisps on to one slice of bread and mash them down so they lie as flat as possible. Rogue crisps will poke into the roof of your mouth so make sure you take the extra time to get them lying flat. Lay the other slice of bread on top of the crispy one so that it looks like a sandwich, then serve on a circular plate.

GUILT
IS
A
WASTED
EMOTION

Apple Energy
BITES

If you like cake, biscuits, apples, sugar and gluten then you are going to love these healthy bites. They're perfect for when your inner snack monster comes out and they make a great pre- or post-workout snack to really get your blood sugar levels pumping. ASDA is one of my favourite resources for quick, delicious produce and they're really on to a winner with these fruity bites.

SERVES 4

INGREDIENTS

4 ASDA apple turnovers

METHOD

Drive to your nearest ASDA. Your bites will taste better if they're locally sourced so download the ASDA app to make sure you're visiting your closest outlet. Purchase a packet of apple turnovers. Sit in the car park and eat them while they're hot.

Chocolate-dipped
BANANAS

Some people say that fruit is nature's candy and this statement rings so true with these delicious bananas. Some people like to use dark chocolate but I find that it's bitter and doesn't quite complement the unique foamy taste of this yummy fruit. My favourite foam bananas come from a pick 'n' mix stand at Liverpool Street Station but your local cinema should have a good substitute.

SERVES 5

INGREDIENTS

1 slab milk chocolate

10 foam bananas

10 cocktail sticks

METHOD

Put the chocolate in a bowl and place it on top of a pan of simmering water, making sure that the water doesn't touch the bowl. While you're waiting for the chocolate to melt, skewer the foam bananas on the cocktail sticks. When the chocolate is melted, dip the foam bananas halfway into the chocolate, then place them on a tray covered in baking parchment. When they're all done, put them in the fridge to cool.

Mains

Main meals are very important because they have to be filling, but they also need to be healthy and delicious. When I started this new way of eating my main concern was deprivation. Will I be hungry? Will I miss my favourite indulgent foods? The answer, thankfully, is no. In this chapter I'll be teaching you how to make some of your favourite staple meals more healthy by swapping out your usual ingredients for nutritious alternatives. You'll be amazed by the range of dishes you can still enjoy as part of this diet. Don't think you can give up carby favourites like pasta or pizza? Think again. Once you've tried these healthy alternatives you'll be wondering why you haven't always eaten this way. Try testing out these recipes on friends and family and show them that nutritious means delicious. Your body and your mind will thank you.

Pizza
PIE

Whenever I tell people about my diet, they are guaranteed to ask one thing: can I still eat pizza? I am so pleased to say 100 per cent yes. You can eat pizza, but not as you know it. I am so inspired by other chefs using quinoa to make pizza bases, but I never eat a food I can't pronounce. If you're trying to cut carbs, and not with a bread knife, I am here to help with this delicious pizza alternative that packs in all the nutrition but isn't missing any of the flavour. The first thing you'll notice in this recipe is that I have changed the base from bread to biscuits. This means that the focus of the meal is not bread. Clever, right? You can use any toppings you like; in this version, instead of tomato sauce, I recommend Marshmallow Fluff, peanut butter or my go-to staple, chocolate nut butter.

SERVES 3

INGREDIENTS

1 packet ginger nut biscuits
1 pat of butter
1 jar Marshmallow Fluff
A selection of your favourite chocolates
1 bag of chocolate drops

METHOD

Empty the packet of ginger nuts and the pat of butter into a food processor and blast until you have the consistency of dough. It should taste rich and sugary, but don't eat it yet! Raw food is healthy and delicious but the finished pizza is worth the wait. Spread the 'dough' on to a tray in a flat, circular shape then spoon on the entire contents of the Marshmallow Fluff jar. Arrange your toppings as desired before finishing the pizza with a scattering of delicious chocolate drops over the top.

Cauliflower
RICE

I love rice but sometimes I find that it can be a bit heavy, especially when I've eaten a lot of it. Cauliflower rice is such a brilliant alternative to white rice because it's low in carbohydrates and lighter than its starchy alternative. It also goes extremely well with this delicious cheese sauce. One of my favourite sayings is 'if in doubt, add cheese', and this little tip is perfect for this dish. I can really tell if my recipes are good by testing them on my brother. Trying to get him to eat healthy food can be an uphill struggle but when I serve him my cauliflower rice he always comes back for seconds.

SERVES 1

INGREDIENTS

½ a head of cauliflower
500g ready-grated cheese

METHOD

Grate your cauliflower on a cheese grater until you have a pile of grains that look a lot like rice. Arrange the grains in a bowl and then microwave them for 1 minute. Pour your ready-grated cheese on to the rice and put it back in the microwave for 1 minute. When you take it out, the cheese should be melted and the cauliflower rice should be saturated with it. I love this dish; it's so warm and nourishing.

One of my favourite sayings is 'if in doubt, add cheese'.

Chocetti

Spiralizers, spiralizers, spiralizers. It seems you can't move for recipes that use this quick-fix gadget. I love using it to make delicious pasta alternatives, but please be warned! It can be very tricky to clean chocolate out of a spiralizer and that means it can be a bit wasteful. It's also potentially dangerous; once I spiralized my finger *and* my sponge while attempting to clean a spiralizer.

Always make sure that you use locally sourced chocolate bars – the corner shop is usually best. Spiralizing can be quite tiring, so make sure that you carb load before you start.

SERVES 1

INGREDIENTS

4 of your favourite chocolate bars

METHOD

Place the chocolate in the spiralizer and turn it clockwise using circular motions. If you want your chocetti to have a bit of crunch, why not add some delicious nuts? Make sure they have been roasted in honey or covered in chocolate. Raw nuts are tasteless and lack delicious salt. Arrange the spiralized chocolate in your most attractive crockery to achieve the full effect.

Top tip: Spiralizing the chocolate can cause it to get caught up in all sorts of places, but I find that any off-spray can be used as a delicious natural body scrub.

Courgetti
TEMPURA

One of the questions I've asked myself a lot when choosing ingredients to include in this book is, 'Will it deep fat fry?' My deep fat fryer is my kitchen's multitasker and I try to use it as often as possible. You'd be amazed at how many dishes benefit from being deep fried in oil. My deep fat fryer and my spiralizer are two of my favourite kitchen gadgets and the chance to use them together on this dish was just too good to miss. Courgetti is such a great healthy alternative to pasta and the batter in this dish really brings it to life. Sweet chilli dipping sauce is one of my favourite condiments because it's full of sugar and MSG, and it adds a vibrant pop of colour to any dish.

SERVES 2

INGREDIENTS

1 cup flour
100ml milk
1 egg
2 courgettes
Sweet chilli dipping sauce

METHOD

Preheat your deep fat fryer to the highest setting. Mix together the flour, milk and egg in a bowl, beating them with a hand-held whisk until you have a rich, creamy batter. Put one end of the courgette in the spiralizer and turn clockwise, until you have ribbons of courgette. Dip the spiralized courgette into the batter then carefully drop it into the deep fat fryer. Remove the courgetti when the batter has become golden and crispy.

Raw Vegan BURGER

A vegan burger is an absolute staple in any plant-based diet and this one is brilliant because it is super-filling and delicious, and completely meat free. Mushrooms are like nature's beef patty and these ones have the added bonus of being rolled in super-nourishing coconut. Coconuts are brimming with electrolytes and are super-good for your metabolism, so this burger really is completely guilt free.

SERVES 1

INGREDIENTS

1 bread roll

Marshmallow Fluff

A handful of coconut mushrooms

METHOD

If you put the word 'raw' in front of something, it automatically makes it healthy; even better, my raw vegan burger involves no skill and no cooking at all. To start, slice open a bread roll. Spread it with marshmallow fluff and arrange the coconut mushrooms on top. It should look just like a New York deli sandwich – but full of healthy goodness.

Mushrooms are like nature's beef patty and these ones have the added bonus of being rolled in super-nourishing coconut.

Healthy Light
RISOTTO

I've always loved risotto but I find it a bit heavy to eat and time-consuming to make, especially at lunch time. Puffed rice provides the perfect lighter alternative, especially because it is already pre-flavoured with delicious sugar, so takes no time at all to make. This is a great dish to serve at a dinner party or to enjoy all by yourself. It's so versatile and looks really impressive – just don't tell anyone how easy it is. Your secret's safe with me!

SERVES 1

INGREDIENTS

600g frosted puffed rice

200ml cow's milk

A handful of marshmallows

METHOD

Pour the puffed rice into a bowl. It should be about halfway up to the bowl's edge. Pour in the milk, being careful not to splash. You'll hear a pleasant crackling that will tell you the puffed rice is almost ready to eat. Scatter the marshmallows on top then eat immediately before the risotto gets soggy. Delicious.

Black Rice
RISOTTO

Sometimes I like to make black rice risotto because it uses black rice instead of white rice. I like to mix up the colours of my carbohydrates because a balanced diet is all about incorporating as many colours as possible. That's why I make so much effort to eat lots of green foods. Black rice is dense with nutrients and totally yummy. Once you've got the hang of this recipe I'm sure you'll come back to it again and again.

SERVES 5

INGREDIENTS

1 box chocolate puffed rice

1 l cow's milk

METHOD

Pour the chocolate puffed rice in equal measure into 5 bowls. Make sure that it doesn't come too close to the brim or there won't be space for the milk and you'll have a chocolate tsunami on your hands – not ideal. Carefully pour the milk on to the chocolate puffed rice until it reaches the brim of your bowl. You should hear a pleasant crackling sound and start to see the milk turn a chocolatey brown colour. This means that the risotto is ready to eat.

Liquorice
NOODLES

I absolutely love Italian food, and giving it up was never an option for me. I think that this twist on a classic is even better than the original, and you'd never believe that it's actually really good for you. Although I did really love gluten, eating pasta every night was giving me really bad IBS. That's why I decided it was time to get creative with this delicious wheat-free alternative. There are lots of ways to create delicious black pasta. Some people use squid ink or seaweed, but I prefer the sweet taste of liquorice. This dish is so full of colour and flavour, and it keeps for days – perfect for a weekday lunch or a snack on a trip to the theatre.

SERVES 2

INGREDIENTS

500g black liquorice

1 bag of liquorice allsorts

METHOD

Unravel the black liquorice into strips, then cut it into 10cm-long laces. Arrange the laces in a bowl so that it has the look of spaghetti; make sure it can easily be twizzled on to a fork. Add the liquorice allsorts and gently toss them with the spaghetti. They should be evenly spaced among the laces. This gives the dish a depth of flavour and a splash of colour that really takes it to the next level, plus it's a great way to get important minerals into your diet.

FREE GLUTEN

The addition of *t*ruffles adds a real depth of flavour and makes the dish feel glamorous and indulgent.

Indulgent Truffle
STRAWGHETTI

Strawghetti is one of my favourite recipes to cook for friends because it really satisfies my sweet tooth. It's also a wonderful pasta alternative that doesn't call for a spiralizer, which can be a nightmare to wash up. The addition of truffles adds a real depth of flavour and makes the dish feel glamorous and indulgent – two very important factors when you're entertaining. My local budget supermarket has been a godsend when it comes to finding rarer, more exotic ingredients. I love knowing that I'll find things there that I won't find anywhere else. The base flavour of this dish is delicious strawberry, a fruit that's packed with vitamins and antioxidants. I think you'll be coming back to this amazing recipe again and again.

SERVES 4

INGREDIENTS

2 packets strawberry laces (non-fizzy)

1 box strawberry truffles

4 cubes white cooking chocolate

METHOD

Empty both packets of strawberry laces and pull apart any strands that may have become stuck together. Arrange them into 4 piles in 4 bowls; you should aim for a swirl formation, with a small nest-like space at the top. Open the box of truffles and select 3 to put in each strawghetti nest. Use a cheese grater to grate the white chocolate on top of the strawghetti for a really sweet finish.

Juices

Green Goodness
JUICE

Green juice is excellent because it's cleansing and energizing and can give you a morning boost without the need for caffeine. This one from Gordon's is my absolute favourite because of its uplifting hints of juniper. Mix with quinine to change things up.

Energizing Blue
JUICE

Blue juice is full of electrolytes and is perfect if you've got a case of the Sunday blues. It's full of sugar to give you a much-needed head rush and its blue flavour makes it really stand apart. This isn't one for the Nutribullet, though – you don't want to lose that delectable fizz.

Green juice is excellent because it's cleansing and energizing and can give you a morning boost without the need for caffeine.

Refreshing Orange JUICE

Orange juice is something from my childhood that I still love. This special version is made in Scotland using natural flavourings to give it a taste not dissimilar to rusty nails. Nothing makes me feel at home more than washing down some warming porridge in the morning with this delicious beverage. Yum.

Coconut WATER

Coconut water is full of electrolytes and provides the perfect kick-start to an energized day. Drinking this version with delicious added Malibu is my second favourite thing to do on the beach, after headstands, so it's a must-have in the summer. I find that this drink works best when it's served with ice. You can either buy ice from your local corner shop or make it yourself, using water and a freezer.

Pick-me-up
PURPLE JUICE

Purple juices are great because they are wintry and warming. Lots of people like to use beetroot in their purple juices but my secret is a glass of cheeky Vimto. The bubbles are so energizing and it has just the right amount of sugar to perk me up after a workout.

Ingredients Arranged in Bowls

This chapter is really symbolic of the way I learned to appreciate and understand food. Learning to arrange ingredients in bowls is the first step to becoming the chef you've always wanted to be. These recipes might be simple and take no experience, time or palate, but they are healthy, and that's the most important step to becoming a better, brighter you.

A carefully arranged bowl is a great way to separate ingredients that don't go together, so you can enjoy each one on its own nutritious merit. I like to make sure that my bowls are packed with vitamins, minerals and antioxidants. When you're eating an abundance bowl, you are eating your own personal smorgasbord of health.

Chocolate
ABUNDANCE BOWLS

People always ask me what my go-to recipes are, and I always tell them that nothing is better than an abundance bowl when your back's against the wall. I call these dishes 'abundance bowls' because they're abundant with joy, and this recipe is one of my all-time favourites. It's not only simple and delicious; it's also realistic and achievable.

This recipe is so easy because all you have to do is arrange the ingredients in a bowl. It's almost not even a recipe! When I first started on my journey, my lack of chef skills held me back, but with a bit of trial and error, I'm now arranging all sorts of things in bowls. I've never looked back.

SERVES 4

INGREDIENTS

16 squares of milk chocolate

32 chocolate caramels

4 caramel wafer bars

4 pack Mini Jaffa Cakes

METHOD

Gently unpackage all the ingredients except for the caramel wafer bars and divide them into four equal portions. Break up the milk chocolate into two-square pieces and place them in a bowl alongside eight chocolate caramels. Nestle a caramel wafer bar, still in its wrapper, between the chocolate caramels and the milk chocolate, then garnish with a lidless packet of Mini Jaffa Cakes.

BOWL

This delicious, nourishing berry bowl is the perfect antidote to wintry weather. It's so quick and easy to arrange and the tiny ready-made milk bottles mean that no nuts need to be blended with water and passed off as milk – result! This recipe is packed with vitamins and nutrients; if your immune system needs a boost, then this is the perfect breakfast for you. As an added bonus, it's easy to prepare in advance, which makes it the perfect breakfast for when you're on the go.

SERVES 1

INGREDIENTS

1 packet gummy milk bottles

1 packet gummy raspberries

1 packet gummy blackberries

METHOD

This recipe is all about freshness, using seasonal berries and nourishing milk to make a naturally healthy meal. Place the delicious milk bottles, blackberries and raspberries in a bowl and make sure that you can see all the ingredients. I like to use blackberries and raspberries but you can change things up depending on what's in season. Milk bottles are a great dairy alternative and keep longer than normal milk so you'll always have them to hand when a berry bowl is just what you feel like.

White Carbs
FOUR WAYS
ABUNDANCE BOWL

This recipe is one of the first abundance bowls I ever attempted and I keep coming back to it. Being able to arrange ingredients in bowls is the most important step you'll take in your food journey, because nothing ruins a recipe like a bad photo on Instagram. The ingredients are the star of the show in this dish, so make sure that you choose them carefully. White carbohydrates are a staple in my food ethos; get ready to use them a lot.

SERVES 1

INGREDIENTS

500g white rice

A handful of oven chips (any brand)

Lashings of butter

1 slice white bread

1 packet of crisps

METHOD

Pre-heat the oven to 190°C. Place the rice in a saucepan, then cover it with boiling water and put it on the hob to boil. Put the oven chips on a baking tray and place the tray in the oven. Butter a piece of bread then fold it in half into a triangular shape. Cut the triangle in half and arrange the 2 sandwiches in a bowl. After 15 minutes, remove the chips from the oven and drain the rice. Use the rice and the chips to fill the rest of the bowl.

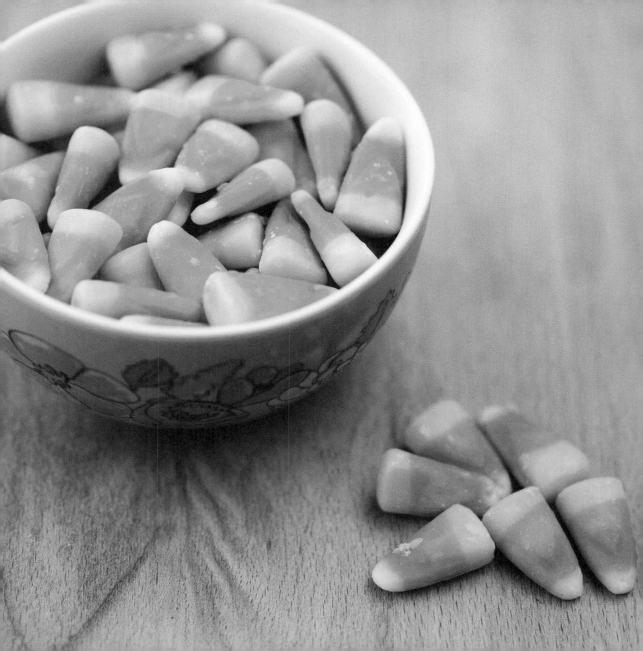

Vibrant Sweetcorn
RAINBOW BOWL

I learned about this delicious sweetcorn recipe when I was on a 'wellness' course in Los Angeles where I was encouraged to eat ice and dust and spend more money than I had on vitamins. Luckily, this delicious sweetcorn is both affordable and abundant with vitamins so it's the perfect immune booster for when the colder weather sets in. It is one of my absolute favourites for autumn. It's so warming and seasonal, and the colours remind me of beautiful autumn leaves. I like to buy my sweetcorn off the cob but, if you've got the time or want a more authentic feel, you can buy it on a cob, or even build it into a cob yourself.

SERVES 2

INGREDIENTS

600g candy corn

METHOD

Pour the candy corn into 2 bowls, making sure to separate it equally so that nobody feels short-changed. Separate the kernels of corn into different colours and arrange them in lines across the bowl. When you're finished it should look like a rainbow, full of vitamins and minerals.

Scrumptious
SHELLFISH SALAD BOWL

Shellfish, for me, feels so indulgent. It's the only thing I want to eat when I visit my parents' summer house by the sea. Responsible, sustainable fishing is so important, so make sure you're eating something that's plentiful and fresh. If you haven't got your sea legs, make sure that you get your produce from an excellent fisherman. I get these from my local budget supermarket; these guys have got it nailed with their seafood platters.

SERVES 2

INGREDIENTS

2 boxes chocolate sea shells

METHOD

Unwrap the tray of sea shells and remove each shellfish individually. Check that the seafood is good to eat by making sure that none of it has melted or is showing signs of discolouration. Nobody wants to be tackling a bout of food poisoning during beach yoga. Once you've inspected your shellfish, arrange them in a beautiful bowl and enjoy.

WORSE THINGS HAVE HAPPENED AT SEA

Brilliant Biscuit
BOWL

This biscuit bowl might just be the best lunch ever because all the ingredients come from one tin; it reminds me of school staff rooms and old ladies. It's perfect for packed lunches on the go, and looks really impressive when you're entertaining. Nobody needs to know that all you've done is arrange the ingredients in a bowl. The pink wafers are my favourite part of this dish. I could just eat trays and trays of them. They're so filling yet light as air, so you can feel really virtuous after enjoying this.

SERVES 4

INGREDIENTS

1 biscuit selection tin

METHOD

Take 4 bowls and divide the biscuits evenly between them. In each biscuit bowl you should have a jammie dodger, a chocolate digestive, an oaty biscuit and a pink wafer. Overlap the biscuits so that they are all neatly arranged in the bowl, and you've got a feast ready for any occasion, from lunch in the office to a dinner party at home.

Nobody needs to know that all you've done is arrange the ingredients in a bowl.

Rejuvenating
VEG BOWL

This bowl is so rejuvenating and nourishing. These vegetables from Choc on Choc are my top find this year – they taste so rich and delicious, I actually love them. If you struggle to get your five-a-day, then this is the recipe for you. This one beautiful bowl includes all the vitamins and minerals you need to get the glow; it's my favourite recipe to turn to when I need to feel refreshed.

SERVES 1

INGREDIENTS

1 chocolate cauliflower

1 chocolate sweetcorn

1 chocolate onion

1 chocolate asparagus

1 chocolate mushroom

2 chocolate carrots

METHOD

This recipe is so easy and delicious, literally anyone can make it. The chocolate vegetables come ready prepared from the market and all it takes is a good eye for arranging ingredients to create a wonderful dish. To start, unwrap your punnet of chocolate vegetables and set them aside. Get a bowl out of the cupboard and arrange the vegetables in it, making sure you don't handle them for too long. You don't want them to melt.

Desserts

I think that this chapter could be my favourite in this book. My mother always said to never trust a woman who thinks that fruit is a pudding, and I've tried to stay true to that ethos when constructing these delicious sweet treats. I do use a lot of fruit in my puddings, but I think that these clever recipes taste so good that you might not notice you're eating fruit at all.

I've always had a sweet tooth, for as long as I can remember, but when I started on this journey, I knew I could not let that stand in my way. That's why all these recipes have been sweetened in the most natural way possible, using healthy, naturally occurring sugars and innovative techniques to make them every bit as indulgent as your favourite desserts. Throughout this chapter you'll learn a range of techniques, from stirring and scattering to drizzling and dipping. Don't be intimidated by these methods: if at first you don't succeed, practice will always make perfect. And nothing tastes better than reaching for something sweet and knowing that it's completely guilt free.

Toffee APPLES

Since becoming a wellness guru, I've really learned the importance of healthy food masquerading as cake. I have also learned that everything tastes better with added sugar. Apples are an excellent source of vitamin C and full of energizing electrolytes, but it's the toffee that really shines in this dish. Autumn is my favourite season because it's the spiritual home of toffee apples. It's also cold enough to wear jumpers. Jumpers are amazing because nobody looks fat in a jumper. In fact, I think it's impossible to put on weight when you're wearing a jumper.

SERVES 6

INGREDIENTS

6 apples

6 sticks

400g sugar

4 tbsp golden syrup

4 tbsp water

METHOD

Skewer the apples on the sticks so they are easy to dip in the toffee. The toffee can get really hot so be careful not to get any on your hands when you're dipping. Boil the sugar and the water in a pan until it forms a liquid caramel consistency and slowly stir in the golden syrup. Roll the apples in the gooey mixture. Put them on some baking parchment to cool.

Strawberry
SMOOTHIE BOWL

Smoothie bowls are so amazing because they combine two of my favourite things – drinking delicious, nourishing juices and arranging ingredients in bowls. This one is packed with delicious sugar and dairy, and helps me feel joyful and energized before a busy day of beach yoga. As I've mentioned before, I'm not a chef, so when I first started arranging my smoothie bowls they were a bit of a mess. Don't worry if you struggle with mixing with a spoon at first – practice makes perfect! It took me months of practice and a trained food stylist to get my toppings to look this good. And remember – whatever you do, don't add chia seeds.

SERVES 1

INGREDIENTS

1 packet Delight
300ml milk
1 tube white chocolate stars
1 tube golden nuggets
3 gummy strawberries

METHOD

Pour the Delight mixture out of the packet and into a bowl. Make sure you use a separate bowl for mixing as it can get quite messy! Add milk. Make sure that the milk you use is locally sourced and comes from cows – we all know that you can't milk an almond. Whip the mixture until you get a smooth paste then carefully pour it into your most Instagrammable bowl. Perfectly arrange the white chocolate stars, golden nuggets and gummy strawberries so that half of the bowl is left exposed and half is covered with the arranged ingredients. This way people can tell that it's not porridge.

Coconut Chia
PUDDING

Chia pudding is brilliant because you can eat it as a dessert, a snack or even a breakfast. I find that chia pudding can look and taste a lot like frogspawn so in this recipe I've replaced the chia seeds with spherical sweets. The coconut rum gives this recipe a much-needed kick. To finish, add a delicious topping of tinned pineapple chunks to make it feel just like a refreshing piña colada!

SERVES 4

INGREDIENTS

4 jelly cubes
570ml boiling water
285ml cold water
2 shots Malibu coconut rum
1 packet spherical sweets
1 tin pineapple chunks

METHOD

Put 4 jelly cubes in a jar and add the boiling water, stirring until they have dissolved. Add the cold water and Malibu and allow the mixture to cool for 10 minutes. Before the jelly sets, drop the spherical sweets in and watch them slowly glide through the mixture. It should start to take on the appearance of frogspawn, with a jelloid consistency. Top with pineapple chunks and move it to the fridge to set.

Blackberry & Apple
CRUMBLE

Crumble is one of my absolute favourite puddings because it's what my mum always used to make me when I was sad. I was so worried about having to give it up when I started my new way of eating. Foraging is one of my favourite activities; there's nothing I love more than picking my own apples and blackberries in the autumn. Wilkinson's is a great place to start your hunt but if that's too difficult then, again, your local cinema will usually come up trumps. The oaty biscuits used in the crust are available from most good supermarkets. Make sure you get the most expensive maple syrup you can afford. One thing I've learned from my new diet is the more expensive the ingredients, the healthier they are.

SERVES 6

INGREDIENTS

1 packet fizzy apples

1 packet gummy blackberries

4 tbsp maple syrup

1 packet oaty biscuits

METHOD

To make the base of this recipe, empty the packets of fizzy apples and gummy blackberries on to a tray and cover them with the maple syrup to create a gooey consistency. Make sure that you use pure maple syrup; doing so will ensure the finished dish is healthy. Blend the oaty biscuits in a food processor until they're crumbly to the touch then cover the blackberries and apples with this sugary dust. Yum.

#
ITS
A
BROWNIE
NOT
A
BANK
ROBBERY

Bananarama
SMOOTHIE BOWL

Smoothie bowls are what I turn to when I need a blast of health. They're so delicious you could almost forget that they're healthy. Banana is one of my favourite flavours because it's exotic and reminds me of sunshine. Bananas are full of potassium and vitamin C, and I love using them in recipes. Their texture is like nature's glue so they work amazingly in baking as well as in puddings, or even on their own. These foam ones are my favourite because their shelf life is longer than regular bananas and they're great for satisfying my sweet tooth.

SERVES 2

INGREDIENTS

1 packet banana Delight

500ml whole fat milk

6 foam bananas

2 tsp chocolate drops

50g desiccated coconut

METHOD

Pour the Delight mixture and the milk into a mixing bowl and beat with a metal spoon until you get a smooth texture, a little bit thicker than a juice. I suggest you use a metal spoon for the mixing so the flavour is interfered with as little as possible. Once you've beaten the mixture, pour it into crockery of your choice. I find that a blue bowl goes well with the yellow mixture. Flatten the top of the mixture and decorate it with the foam bananas and chocolate drops, then sprinkle with yummy coconut.

Banana and Cacao
CHIA PUDDING

Chia pudding is just the best. I know that I'm going to love a food when it works as both a breakfast and a pudding, and the big bonus here is that it's a superfood! My only problem with chia pudding is that it takes ages to make and looks terrible. That's why this ready-made rice pudding is the perfect alternative. It comes in a tin so it lasts for ages and you only have to heat it up.

SERVES 2

INGREDIENTS

8 foam bananas
4 tins rice pudding
2 tbsp chocolate chips

METHOD

Line 2 jam jars with 4 foam bananas each, pressed vertically against the glass so you can see them. Warm the rice pudding for 5 minutes on a low heat, and then pour the warm pudding mixture into the jam jar, being careful not to disturb the bananas. The bananas are the star of this dish so you want to make sure you can see them. To finish, top the pudding with chocolate drops and get ready to dive in.

This ready-made rice pudding is the perfect alternative.

Health and Beauty Tips

People are always asking me about my beauty regime and I'm so pleased to finally share my secrets. I love natural remedies, and I try to turn to my kitchen cupboards for inspiration as much as possible. You'll be amazed by what you'll find. I've tested everything from golden syrup hair masks to lard moisturizer to create the best natural remedies to make your hair shine and your skin glow.

Drink Now,
THINK LATER

A lot of people swear by drinking cider vinegar in the morning but I say skip the vinegar and just drink cider. There are lots of different varieties of cider so choose whatever works best for you. You should always try to buy the most expensive cider that you can, because expensive food equals healthy food. Cheers!

Another great tip to remember is that it's impossible to put on weight when you're hungover! The same goes for birthdays, wakes or when you're revising for exams. How great is that? My dad once had to ask me to stop eating at a funeral so there would be food for the other guests; the next day I looked and felt so radiant. Proof that these tips really do work!

Natural Lip STAIN

I love natural make-up but I've found that a lot of the brands I've tried keep falling short. That's why I've started going to my kitchen to find gorgeous natural products to make me glow from the inside out. Red wine is truly the most wonderful lip stain. If you drink enough of it, the colour embeds itself in your lips and it lasts for hours. It's also delicious and made from lovely natural grapes, which are packed full of antioxidants to keep your lips moisturized and plump. My favourite shade is Rioja, but Malbec is also great for a deep red.

To get the colour right, drink from a large glass so that the wine can get to all the corners of your mouth. Watch out for red wine fangs, though. Nobody wants to look like they've had an interview with a vampire.

Cacao and Coconut
FACE MASK

I really love natural remedies and this face mask is one of my favourite beauty hacks. It's easy to create at home, using what's in your kitchen cupboards. Coconuts are one of my favourite wonder ingredients. They're so versatile, full of antioxidants and smell really yummy. Coconut chocolate bars are the perfect way to incorporate coconut into your diet and your beauty regime. The addition of cacao provides essential minerals that will give you baby-soft skin.

INGREDIENTS

4 coconut chocolate bars

METHOD

Unwrap the coconut chocolate bars and chop them into small pieces. Each bar should be divisible into about 6. Place the pieces into your food processor and buzz on high for about 2 minutes. You should have a malleable, sticky texture that's ready to get you glowing from the inside out.

Oil
PULLING

Oil pulling is an amazing, natural way to get cleaner, whiter teeth. Lots of people like to use coconut oil but I find the oil a bit sickening so instead I use healthy, nourishing condensed milk. Condensed milk lasts longer than normal cow's milk and it tastes absolutely delicious. It also comes in a perfect toothpaste-like tube so you can put it directly on to your toothbrush.

Since I started using condensed milk, my teeth have never been better and it's so yummy, I even swallow it afterwards. The tubes are brilliant because they're resealable and can be stored easily alongside your toothbrush and toothpaste. Don't forget to floss!

Kitchen Essentials

Almond BUTTER

It's official. I am a nut butter addict and this recipe is what I always reach for if I'm bored of eating ice or dust. It tastes absolutely divine in cookies or on crackers. You can even eat it straight out of the fridge with a spoon. My top tip is to slather it on white bread. Heaven!

SERVES 10

INGREDIENTS

250g block salted butter

20 almonds

METHOD

Take the block of salted butter, unwrap it from the foil and put it on a plate. Individually place almonds in horizontal stripes on to the butter and press down on them gently so they don't move. A little research will tell you that butter comes in a cuboid formation (don't worry if you can't remember your maths GCSE – I know I can't), so you have 6 sides to cover. All the sides need to be decorated symmetrically, so take your time. This dish is as much about how it looks as how yummy it tastes.

You can make your own
stock by boiling up bones
but I prefer to use this
cheeky shortcut.

Bone BROTH

I think that it's time I let you in on one of my best-kept secrets: although I call this recipe bone broth, it's really just another name for stock. You can make your own stock by boiling up bones but I prefer to use this cheeky shortcut. Drinking a bowl of bone broth, for me, is like drinking liquid health. It's full of flavour and nourishing vitamins and minerals. You can pick the ingredients for this broth up from any reputable supermarket so you don't even need to visit expensive health food shops. This is one recipe that you won't be able to do without.

SERVES 4

INGREDIENTS

1 l water

2 stock cubes

METHOD

Boil the water in a kettle then pour into a jug. Unwrap the stock cubes and place them in a bowl. Pour the boiling water over them and stir. Use your bone broth in a dish of your choice or freeze it for a later date.

Water

It might seem silly to you to include a recipe for water, but flavoured water is delicious and anything that makes you drink more of the good stuff is definitely fine by me. You should drink 25 litres of water a day when you're following this diet, which seems like a lot, especially when water doesn't taste of anything. You can use any flavour you like to make your water more interesting but my favourite flavour enhancer is blackcurrant squash. It turns the water a delicious purple colour and pumps it full of vitamin C.

SERVES 1

INGREDIENTS

2 shots blackcurrant squash

1 glass water

METHOD

Pour 2 shots of blackcurrant squash into a glass. Fill the glass with water from your tap. Some people like to use filtered water, which is fine but it can be time consuming to remember to fill up your filter jug. Taste the water to check the strength of flavour and add either water or squash to achieve your desired taste.

A Day in MY LIFE

My life is so amazing. I start every day the same way, with a quick cuddle with my pet dog, Harold. Harold is the perfect pet because he's self-sufficient and will eat anything in his path, just like me. Once I've fed Harold, I make myself a shot of cider and warm water. This kick-starts my metabolism and gets me a bit giddy before my first yoga practice of the day.

I'll practise doing headstands for an hour with my personal yoga instructor and pick a picture to post on Instagram so my followers know what I'm up to. Then I'll take Harold on a walk to my favourite breakfast spot – my local greasy spoon. I'll eat a full English with extra black pudding, before taking Harold to the park. Eggs are an excellent source of protein and the hash brown gives me a burst of energy before my walk. When I'm in the park, depending on the season, I'll either take a picture of some blossom, some autumnal leaves, a sunny sky or Harold frolicking in the snow. After our walk it's time to head back to Stella HQ, making sure to take a picture of the beautiful pastel houses on the way back.

When I'm back at home, it's time for another yoga session with one of my beautiful friends. Most of my friends are wellness gurus so they're always free to practise crabs in the middle of the day. If the weather's good, we'll do our yoga practice outside and top up on vitamin D.

At around 11:30 a.m., I'm finally ready to get down to business. I head down the road to my local produce providers and stock up on ingredients for recipe testing. I

use a lot of fresh ingredients in my recipes so I like to visit the corner shop at the end of my road and my local supermarket to make sure I get the best seasonal produce. In the autumn time I might go foraging in my local cinema's pick 'n' mix stand to find juicy berries.

My chef makes my lunch as I'm usually busy testing recipes, but if I'm not recipe testing, I'll play with Harold until lunch time. For lunch, I usually have ingredients arranged in a bowl, or maybe some nut butter. After lunch I'll get my Nutribullet out and make a cleansing green juice before sitting down to write 57 different uses for coconut oil on my blog.

After lunch I like to take a rejuvenating nap. You can never have too much beauty sleep. When I wake up I'll make some energy balls and do a face mask using ingredients from my kitchen cupboards. Ketchup really helps me to get my sparkle back. At around 4 p.m. I'll start drinking. Red wine is the most amazing natural lip stain so I like to drink quite a lot before I go out.

In the evening, I'll meet my friends at an organic juice bar before squeezing in one more yoga class. By this point I'm usually quite drunk, so I like to go to Bikram yoga, where it's warm enough to have a snooze. Once I've slept off my afternoon booze I go home and cover my body in coconut oil before getting into bed and checking my Instagram one last time.

Meal
PLANS

My food ethos is all about making healthy eating easier and more accessible for everyone. At first, my friends and family were a little daunted by the idea of dairy alternatives like condensed milk and cooking with Malibu coconut water, but since I've introduced them to the joys of sugar and alcohol at breakfast time, I can happily say that I am now preaching to the converted.

    I wanted to share these meal plans with you so you never struggle to think of when to serve my food and what to serve it with. Hopefully these tips will stand you in good stead for entertaining friends, cooking family meals or thinking ahead on busy days.

BRUNCH

Brunch is one of my favourite meals because it completely legitimizes drinking before noon. If you don't want to drain your local café of mimosas and would rather do some entertaining at home, I have the perfect recipes for you. The Berry Blast Breakfast Smoothie always goes down a real treat with guests. The popping candy provides such a delicious surprise, and is great for breaking the ice. Avocado and Eggs on Toast is a perfect first course. My personal preference is to eat savoury before sweet but you can do either/or. The Coconut Chia Pudding is perfects as a breakfast or dessert, and the Malibu makes it work perfectly for brunch. Your friends will never want to go out again!

Berry Blast Breakfast Smoothie, page 30
Avocado and Eggs on Toast, page 18
Coconut Chia Pudding, page 128

KITCHEN SUPPER

For a casual kitchen supper with my friends, I always turn to a one-pot wonder so I don't spend too much time in the kitchen. Risotto is healthy, easy and, most importantly, delicious. It's so easy, you can even ask your guests to pour their own milk. I love it when everyone gets involved in the cooking process. This is a dish that brings friends together so you can share your passion for healthy eating and healthy cooking.

Black Rice Risotto, page 88

DINNER PARTY

Dinner parties are when I really want to impress and show off my glorious healthy food. People are sometimes nervous about coming to one of my dinner parties because they think that health food is boring, but this menu is sure to set the record straight. Three courses might seem like a lot but you can prepare some of these dishes in advance and they look really impressive.

As a starter, I recommend my Seafood Surprise; it's one of my favourite recipes. Cooking with fish can be complicated so I find that this surprisingly simple broth starts off the evening with a showstopper. Make sure you buy your goldfish crackers on the same day that you plan to cook with them so they're as fresh as possible. The broth is served cold.

For the main course, you can't beat Indulgent Truffle Strawghetti. Truffles are so indulgent and show that you really care about top-notch ingredients. Strawghetti is a brilliant pasta alternative because you don't need a spiralizer and it's easy to make for lots of people. I've never met anyone who doesn't love my strawghetti recipe and I hope that you won't either.

Finally, crumble! Crumble is yummy and quick because you can do all the preparation beforehand and just pop it in the oven for 15 minutes before you're ready for pudding. It's such a warming dessert and doesn't taste healthy at all so you'll have smiles all round. My sister has a terrible sweet tooth and she loves my crumble, so I'll take that as proof that this dessert is a winner.

Seafood Surprise, page 36
Indulgent Truffle Strawghetti, page 95
Blackberry & Apple Crumble, page 131

Acknowledgements

First and foremost I would like to thank my followers for sticking with me on my food journey. You have inspired me so much. I only hope that I have inspired you in turn to make every day a cheat day.

Thanks must go out to my co-creator and number-one champion, Faye Stewart. Had she not hired me and allowed me to get away with taking pictures of food all day when I was supposed to be working, I would never have come so far.

I'd like to thank my parents for allowing me to move back in with them to write this book. Special thanks goes out to my mum for keeping a constant supply of WKD on hand. My brother and sisters, Katrina, Francesca and Geordie. Being the younger siblings of a healthy-eating phenomenon such as me cannot be easy, especially when I always get the last Peperami.

I'd like to thank my friends for listening to me drone on about my healthy new diet. I know it's hard to see me looking so foxy all the time, but you should just try to be less jealous.

Thank you to my agent, Caroline, for embracing my food ethos and helping me become the goddess I am today. Also thank you for letting me spiralize cheese in the office. I'll never forget your kindness.

Thank you to everyone at Penguin Random House, particularly my editor, Emily, and my photographer, Issy. I will never forget how I felt when you put jammie dodgers on my eyes.

Finally, I would like to apologize to my dog. I'm sorry that I ate all of your biscuits. I thought they were bone-shaped energy bars. They were delicious.